Honest With God

Poems And Reflections For Worship
And Private Devotions

by

Helen M. Clarke

Contents

Life's Ups And Downs

1. Who Am I?

When I think of all the people
Who have walked this earth before
All the centuries of living
- Who am *I*? One being more

Where do *I* fit in the picture?
Can I justify my place?
Am I valued as a member
Of the worldwide human race?

Do I have a special mission?
Will I play a vital part?
Is my role to fight injustice?
Offer counsel? Warm the heart?

Help me, Lord, to hear my calling
Help me recognise your voice
Show me, please, the way to serve you
Guide me safely through each choice

2. Anger

Are you there? Do you care?
Will you answer my prayer?
Does it matter to you how I'm feeling?
I'm so angry – hurt too
I don't know what to do
If I ask, will you offer me healing?

I need help, I can't cope
Give me peace, give me hope
I don't want to be bitter or snappy
Self-control's at its worst
I'm so tense I could burst
Calm me down, please. I'm really unhappy

3. The Gift Of Life

Life's wonders and riches surround us
Small shoots peeping up through the earth
Wild creatures, whose instincts astound us
The joy at a new baby's birth

Exuberant puppy, so eager
Just being alive is a thrill
And humans – how much we can offer
Through good use of skills and free will

Creativeness, scholarship, service
Crafts, literature, music and art
Togetherness, love and compassion
Kind words and deeds, straight from the heart

And central to life is renewal
In Spring cheerless gardens revive
Birds nest-building, hedgehogs emerging
Buds opening – nature's alive!

We witness resilience daily
Grass fighting its way through a crack
Weeds – stubborn, tenacious, determined
Life won't stop, it keeps bouncing back

It rallies to challenge disaster -
Plants thriving in once barren ground
New life in a desolate wasteland
Fresh hope springing up all around

Life's precious, a gift to be treasured
Respected, and nurtured with care
Each part has its own special value
Let's celebrate life *everywhere*

4. Nightmare World

I had a deeply shocking dream
A long, long time ago
In 1980 – there abouts
Which left me feeling low

The world had changed, and not for good
Strange laws controlled the land
Free speech and independent thought
Had been completely banned

On issues, one official line
One attitude held sway
All other views and values were
Condemned and cast away

Folk weren't allowed to criticise
Harsh comments were a crime
"Judgemental" was a charge to dread
- You'd end up doing time

Bright students were too delicate
To cope with hot debate
And had to be protected from
Beliefs and truths they'd hate

Behaviour was bewildering
No morals seemed to guide
Guilt, fault, responsibility
Were freely laid aside

Now childhood was a concept lost
The experts seemed quite sure
That such indulgence undermined
A country so mature

No time for fun, creative play
No boredom to explore
Just structured learning right from birth
Assessed by daily score

The pressures weighed down heavily
Achievement reigned supreme
Activities for after school
No chance to muse or dream

And parents had no job to do
- Not capable, the claim -
No duty to their offspring
- This would free them from all blame

On diet, hygiene, exercise
Mere parents had no say
On lifestyle, hobbies, discipline
Their choice was snatched away

Yet children, though not free to roam
In case they came to harm
Weren't supervised when safe inside
And this caused no alarm

These mini grown-ups suffered stress
Poor health – the mental kind
Fear, sleep disorders, loneliness
They knew no peace of mind

And people, young and old alike
Instead of friends had *screens*
No interaction face to face
No happy, chatty scenes

Relationships with gadgets were
Obsessive and intense
Addictive, claustrophobic
- And devoid of common sense

These screen friends thrived on nastiness
- Believe it if you will
The practice was to seek out those
Whose gibes would make you ill

And everyone was dressed the same
Man, woman, girl and boy
Identifying gender seemed
To rankle and annoy

No option to be “girly”
Or a tomboy, bold and tough
No gentlemanly chivalry
No macho “blokey” stuff

Yet babies still existed – so
They weren’t all *quite* the same
The neuter image didn’t hold
- A rather puzzling game

Dire warnings were a daily curse
No food was safe to eat
All games and weather posed a threat
- Survival was a feat

… I woke, in sickened, anxious state
How awful life would be
If these things really happened –
Then relief swept over me

My nightmare was a fantasy
No need to fret or weep
It wouldn’t happen – never could!
… I drifted back to sleep

5. Everybody Welcome

Do we welcome people enthusiastically into the Christian fold? Do we make them feel comfortable and give them a sense of belonging? If visitors come to our church, do we greet them warmly, make sure they have everything they need and help them to find somewhere to sit where they don't have to worry about "pinching somebody's place" (which they know is a very real risk, however vehemently we deny it!)?

Or do we ignore them, albeit because we're wary of smothering them, embarrassing them or scaring them off? Do we leave them floundering with a bewildering choice of books and pieces of paper in our anxiety not to seem patronising? Do we sit back and hope they will be able to work everything out for themselves? After all, it's not *that* difficult, is it, if you think about what you're doing? Do we appreciate how daunting a straightforward act of worship can be for someone who doesn't "know the ropes"? Do we come across as self-righteous and intimidatingly devout and confident to someone who is grappling with an embryonic or challenged faith?

When I was in my early twenties a friend of mine, who had recently started going to church with me, asked me whether God spoke to me. Without a second thought I said "Yes", believing this to be the correct Christian response to such a question. My friend was despondent. She claimed she wasn't a proper Christian and never could be. She had never heard God talking. She had never heard His voice. He didn't speak to *her*. She wasn't the right sort of person to be a Christian.

I was shocked that she had taken the idea of God's voice so literally, but also deeply ashamed of my own cowardice and pride. I had never heard God speaking to me. My Christian upbringing had taught me to be constantly *listening* for God, so I assumed that He *did* speak to me, but I had never actually *heard* Him. I had never been aware of being spoken to by God. I told my friend the truth. She was reassured by my confession and continued on her journey of faith.

How relieved I was that she had expressed her disappointment to me and given me the opportunity to discuss the issue with her honestly! That day I realised, for the first time, how easily we can put people off, alienate them, make them feel that Christianity isn't for them.

Christianity *is* for them. It's for everybody. *All* are welcome. Let's make sure everyone knows that.

6. Too Much To Understand

I can't understand, God, why life is so harsh
And sometimes I fear you don't care
That life's full of danger, destruction and woe
And people are filled with despair

I can't understand, God, why nature's so cruel
- Floods, hurricanes, earthquakes, ill health -
Why people are starving, in squalor and drought
While others have comfort and wealth

I can't understand, God, why evil prevails
Why wicked deeds meet with success
Why acts of aggression and terror seem blessed
It scares me, I have to confess

I do understand that you gave us free will
Is that why you don't take control?
And, yes, I'm aware that *you* see the *big* plan
While *I* just see *part* of the whole

And sometimes I sense that things could have been worse
So often when tragedy's struck
Its dreadful potential was yet *more* severe
Divine intervention? Or luck?

I know that earth's living and so, I suppose
Things will move, develop and change
We've done so much damage, we must take some blame
When nature's behaviour seems strange

But people still suffer, this life's all we know
And heartache's so painful to bear
Please help us to feel your compassion and love
And see that you really do care

7. Thank You

For smiling faces, happy voices
Laughter, fun and pleasure
For hobbies, treats and holidays
And special times to treasure

For birdsong, rainbows, scenery
Rich beauty all around us
For fauna, flora – all the joys
Of nature that astound us

For kindness, love and fellowship
Each cause for celebration
For *everything* that warms the heart
Our thanks and adoration

8. Bible Study

I don't need to study the Bible any more. I must know it inside out by now, especially the Gospels. I've lost count of how many times I've read through the Gospels from beginning to end. And I know all the other major stories as well, like Noah's Ark and Jonah and Job, and all that business with David and Goliath and Daniel in the lions' den. No, I don't need to study the Bible any more.

Yet – do you know something strange? Sometimes when I'm sitting in church listening to the Bible reading – or *half* listening to the Bible reading because I don't need to listen to it properly – what I'm hearing doesn't actually sound at all familiar to me. Even when it's from the Gospels. Even allowing for different translations of the Bible. Sometimes a passage of the Bible I have read over and over again takes me by surprise. It makes a point that I don't remember being aware of before. Or I notice a little – yet highly significant – detail that I've never picked up on before. Sometimes, particularly with Old Testament lessons, I'm even left wondering, *did I really know that story, or did I just assume I knew it because I've heard it mentioned so many times? …*

Hmm. Perhaps I *do* need to study the Bible a bit more after all!

9. Please Forgive Me

Please forgive me when I'm selfish
When I'm thoughtless or unkind
When I'm harsh or lack compassion
In my speech or in my mind
When I'm coldly apathetic
Not prepared to take a stand
When I know support is needed
But hold back my helping hand
Please forgive me for my weakness
When I don't do all I could
Grant me courage, strength and wisdom
To behave the way I should

10. To Pray Or Not To Pray

What's the best time of day to reflect and to pray?
In the morning, first thing, when I waken?
Will I focus my mind? Will I drift into dreams?
Would my vague, garbled words be mistaken?

After breakfast, perhaps. Could I find time to pray?
- Do prayers *count* if disjointed and hurried?
If I'm rushing around, if my prayers are "dashed off"
They'll seem shallow and then I'll be worried

In my lunch break, I wonder? There *might* be a chance
If my privacy isn't invaded
Would I have the self-discipline, freshness of mind?
- Or decide I'm too weary and jaded?

In the evening – that's surely a good time for prayer
For devotional thinking and learning
But – well, when I've been busy I want to relax
Self-indulgence, in truth, is my yearning

So it's bedtime – good sound preparation for night
Heartfelt prayers poured out warmly, concisely
- But by then I'm so sleepy. I want to switch off
And a quick "Good-night, God" suits me nicely

What's the best way to pray and reflect on the day?
In instalments, small helpings, brief sessions?
Just a word now and then when life's peaceful and calm
… Observations … entreaties … confessions …

Is there only one way to reflect and to pray?
After all, God can hear us all clearly
He will listen and answer through night *and* through day
He's our solace and loves us all dearly

11. Sorrow

Sadness overwhelms me
Sorrow fills my heart
A dreadful sense of emptiness
Is tearing me apart

Life feels flat, oppressive
Darkness fills my soul
I'm in a lonely vacuum
Over which there's no control

Reach me, please, Lord Jesus
Fill me with your peace
I need to feel your loving strength
Please give my pain release

12. In It Together

When I think of all the decades and generations and centuries that have already passed, and of all the millions of people who inhabited the earth during those eons of existence, it strikes me that there is something very special about those who are in the world at the same time as we are. There is something particularly precious about those who share our lives with us. Our family and friends. Our neighbours, colleagues and fellow worshippers. This feeling extends to animals too. Think of all those pets – real little people in our lives.

We're all here together. Now. In this place. For better or worse. Faced with the same challenges and issues, possibilities and dangers, hopes and fears. We're in it together, in this ever-changing, ever-complex world, striving – for the most part – to make the best we can of it.

In my most charitable and sentimental moments I feel a rush of warmth even for people, with certain exceptions, I struggle to appreciate on a day-to-day basis.

We're here together. Let's *enjoy* being here together. Let's make *our* age a good one for the world.

13. Thrown Together

How many million creatures
Dwellers of land, sky and sea
How many million people
Lived on this earth before me?

How many eons of living
How much existence has been?
How many share the world with me?
… How few of these I have seen!

When I reflect on the numbers
One question comes to the fore
- How did *we* end up together?
Here? *Now*? – It's hard to ignore

People we know, those unheard of
People we see from afar
Those on our screens, in our papers
Just think how *special* they are!

Folk of this age, thrown together
Thousands of years have gone by
Yet here *we* are, thrown together
How did it happen? And why?

Loved ones. Friends, neighbours, relations
Colleagues, acquaintances, friends
Rivals, those feared, fellow Christians
Part of *our* world and its trends

When I survey those around me
Sometimes it moves me to tears
- Feeling we're in this together
Fills me with warmth for my peers

Let's make life good for each other
Let's make *our* age one to prize
Let's leave a mark to be proud of
Our age – "The Age of the Wise"

14. A Prayer For Strength

Please help me keep going when life seems hard work
And nothing I do reaps reward
When trying seems pointless and energy's low
And most of my efforts ignored

Please help me be patient when things are too slow
And waiting's so hard to endure
When, tense and frustrated, I over-react
Demanding to *have* and be *sure*

Please help me be calm when anxiety strikes
And worries and doubts flood my mind
When panic and fear weaken reason and faith
And peace isn't easy to find

Please help me be pleasant and treat people well
When inside I'm angry or hurt
Remembering others have feelings and needs
Please help me be friendly, not curt

And please, Lord, forgive me when in my distress
I blame you for things that go wrong
- Unkind accusations, objections, complaints -
Please help me be loving and strong

15. Whether We Like It Or Not

Sometimes it doesn't seem fair, Lord. We're stuck in this world, whether we like it or not, through no fault of our own, and there is so much expected of us. There is so much demanded of us. We're under constant pressure. Pressure to make a success of our lives. Pressure to earn a living. Pressure to justify our existence. Pressure to make judgements and decisions when, as often as not, we don't fully understand the implications of our choices. Pressure to solve problems and deal with complications. Pressure to cope with the terrible things going on around us as well as with our own day-to-day difficulties.

Sometimes this all weighs too heavily on me and I feel as if I no longer have the strength or energy to struggle on. I don't feel as if I can keep going any longer. Other people manage. We're all in the same boat. We're all stuck in this world, whether we like it or not, through no fault of our own. It's not just me. Please help me to rise above self-pity and break away from my self-absorption and find a way to live a worthy life.

16. Special Occasion

We thank you for the blessings
Of this very special day
For all the love and joy we share
Be part of us, we pray

17. Misfit

I sometimes don't feel I belong in this world
There's so much that doesn't seem right
So much that distresses, offends and annoys
Please comfort me, Lord, in my plight

I know I'm quite fussy in things I don't like
Some might say I'm stuck in a rut
I cling to my values, react against change
Hate scandal, bad language and smut

On TV so much is unpleasant and crude
Sex, gambling, drugs, attitudes tough
Brutality, drunkenness, bitterness, strife
- In real life there's trouble enough!

Abuse, acts of terror, scams, wars, messed up lives
Technology ousting the brain
All-powerful experts with no common sense
Aggressive expansion and gain

Please help me to know how I fit in this world
And understand what I should do
Accept it or challenge it? Go with the flow?
I'm lost. I need guidance from you

18. People Problems

Sometimes I despair of human nature. People drive me to distraction. It's not that I'm misanthropic. I love people. I really do. But people are *so frustrating*. So much so that I become quite despondent at times. The way they behave and react, getting upset and angry (and yes, I know I do too) when surely it would be better to rise above the problem or see the funny side of it. How hard we find it to keep things in perspective! How hard we find it to get outside our own feelings and attitudes and consider how our behaviour or reactions might affect other people – bickering, careless and thoughtless behaviour that causes accidents, anxiety, heartache and tragedy.

There is so much misery and pain, resentment and bitterness in the world and, sadly, there always will be. How can we avoid it when we're never-endingly behaving and reacting in ways that hurt people? I don't want to control other people. I have no desire to do that at all. Yet there are times when I desperately want to control their behaviour and the way they respond to things. How often do we try to calm someone down, but to no effect? How often do we urge people to come to terms with something, to "not let it get to you. It's not worth it"? And how many times do our comments have any positive impact?

People are *so frustrating*!

19. Free Will

When God gave us free will
Did He know what we'd do?
Did He guess we'd abuse it so badly?
Was He blinded by hope?
Did He trust us too much?
Does He watch us and shake His head sadly?

When we're mean and cause pain
Does He yearn to press STOP?
When we're thoughtless, destructive, uncaring
Is He tempted to tweak us?
Retune us? Rewind?
Do we leave Him distressed and despairing?

When we damage His world
When we throw back His love
Is He filled with regret and misgiving?
Did He make a mistake
When He gave us free will?
Can't we show Him He's right by fair living?

20. Fear

I'm so scared I feel sick
I can't face what's ahead
My heart's aching. The future looks bleak
When awake I crave sleep
But at night I just weep
Nothing gives me the comfort I seek

Lord, please help me to cope
Let me know that you're there
With me always, aware of my pain
Give me courage and strength
Help me see through the tears
That my trust in you isn't in vain

21. Faith, Trust, Complacency

You know I'm a worrier, Lord. You know I fret and panic and torment myself over the slightest little thing. I can't seem to discriminate between reasonable concern and irrational anxiety. I just worry regardless.

It wears me down. It wears my loved ones down. It must wear you down too. You must wonder why I can't just trust you as I should. You must wonder why I sabotage my own happiness by compulsively finding something to dread, even in the safest and most joyful of situations. Why can't I put my faith in you? Why do I find it so much easier to worry than to trust you?

Is it because I'm scared of what trust in you involves? Is it that underlying fear that what *you* have in mind isn't necessarily the same as what *I* have in mind? Is that why I can't allow myself to place everything in your hands? Am I too apprehensive and self-protective about what I would be letting myself in for?

I *want* to trust you. I so desperately want to trust you and have faith in you, but I don't know where the line is between having faith and taking it for granted that everything will be all right. Faith isn't a magic wand, much as I would like it to be. Faith doesn't guarantee me freedom from heartache and suffering. Faith doesn't mean everything will happen exactly the way I want it to.

So what *is* faith? And how do I know I can trust you when you won't promise me that I won't have to suffer? How can I trust and have faith – and really feel the comfort of that – without the certainty that things will work out the way I feel I need them to?

Please help me. It's a struggle and I don't know how to change.

22. Good Versus Evil

Good will conquer evil
Good will find a way
Evil deeds and wickedness
Will never win the day

Love holds us together
Hatred has no role
After great atrocities
Compassion takes control

People pull together
Helpful, caring, kind
Evil will be overcome
And hatred undermined

23. The World Through The Window

When down at heart, what lifts your spirits?
I stand by the window and gaze
The world of our overgrown garden
Can brighten the darkest of days

An old plastic tub full of water
Plus pondweed, a stone and a log
- An eyesore for certain, but precious -
Is home to a large, handsome frog

And each time I glance through the window
I check for a weed-covered bump
For frog loves to hang in the water
Or sit on the log, primed to jump

And as for the birds – what a blessing!
They cheer me, whatever my mood
My dear, hungry friends – how rewarding
To watch them come down for their food

Doves, starlings, tits, dunnocks – one robin
The sparrows, so cheeky and smart
And blackbird, so focused and busy
Two bullfinches, never apart

And let's not forget Outlaw Squirrel
Who moves with such beauty and grace
Those neat little hands – how exquisite
And what an adorable face!

So if you feel down, look around you
Or listen, quite still, for a while
There's sure to be something that pleases
That comforts or forces a smile

24. Forgiveness

Forgiveness is one of the fundamental rules of Christian living. Jesus stressed its importance on more than one occasion. Yet it isn't always easy to forgive, especially when we're very angry or have been badly hurt. Sometimes we want to hold on to our rage and nurse our grievances. We can't let go. We won't let go. We have no desire to let go. Perhaps we feel that forgiving those who have wronged us will somehow compromise our status as innocent victims. Offering forgiveness – letting go – can feel like a denial of the severity of the offence, suggesting that it was only a minor slip-up and doesn't really matter.

Most of us are neither evil nor uncaring but, even so, we still make mistakes. We still suffer deep regret from time to time for our actions or words. Just imagine if we could never be forgiven. How awful it would be! How unbearable and lonely it would be if everyone we had ever offended, deliberately or accidentally, refused to forgive us.

It takes strength and grace to forgive. It takes courage to cast off the prop of justified resentment and move forward without it, unsupported by it. However, resentment leads to bitterness. Bitterness leads to hatred. And hatred achieves nothing positive. Hatred is destructive and poisonous. It sours all areas of life for the person it is controlling. It causes that person to hurt others. There is no place for hatred in the Christian heart. It goes against everything Jesus taught us and it certainly isn't healthy to allow festering wounds to eat away at us.

Please, Lord, for our own sakes and for the sake of others, help us to forgive.

Through The Year

25. A New Year Prayer

It's scary, this big occasion. I don't find it exciting, this stark reminder that time is rushing on and there's nothing I can do about it. I find it threatening, sinister even. Why do people celebrate something so ominous?

A fresh start? Yes, I can see that, especially if the previous year has been an unpleasant one, but all this talk of not knowing what's ahead, what the coming year has in store for us - well, it terrifies me. While I cling sentimentally to the last dregs of a Christmas that many have already put behind them, I fill myself with dread. My comforting plans for next Christmas – which will be perfect – turn into heart-rending speculation about the future. Will my loved-ones still be here next Christmas? Will *I* still be here next Christmas? Was this my final chance to make Christmas perfect and I failed to do so?

No. I don't like New Year – not without the assurance that everything will be all right and nothing bad will happen to anyone.

Please help me come to terms with uncertainty. Please give me the courage to face the unknown. Please give me the strength to move forward with hope and strength.

26. New Year

New year. New hope. New aims. New plans
Life won't stop moving on
What's passed is with us, in our hearts
But still the old year's gone

We're moving on - we have no choice
We can't turn back the clock
We carry forward all we've known
Reflect, perhaps, take stock

New year. New dreams. New challenges
Life ushers us along
New skills discovered, wisdom gained
Life's motion makes us strong

27. Giving Up Lent?

Do I think about Lent?
Do I take it on board?
Do I give it attention? – Not really
Do I learn? Do I grow?
Does it strengthen my faith?
Does my knowledge of self deepen yearly?

To my shame, I'm aware
That Lent comes … then it goes
And I celebrate Easter with gladness
As to Lent – what was *that*?
Forty days – doing *what*?
… Does my lack of thought fill me with sadness?

Did I give something up?
Did I take something on?
Did I look at myself with misgiving?
Did I change? Or reflect?
Look ahead with new hope?
See the need for a fresh way of living?

What *is* Lent all about
For a person like me?
For a Christian who takes things for granted?
Do I feel it at all?
Does it *touch* me at least?
Has the seed of renewal been planted?

28. Are We Like The Crowd?
(*Palm Sunday*)

The cheering crowd, the jeering crowd
How quickly moods can alter!
How easily we're influenced
How soon convictions falter!

The entry to Jerusalem
Triumphal, strong, though humble
With palm-strewn roads and praising throng
Who'd guess such faith would crumble?

Yet not long after, "Crucify!"
The stirred up people chanted
Manoeuvred - brain-washed – threatened – swayed
Their new request was granted

Are *we* that fickle, changeable?
Does faith depend on glory?
Do *we* give way when pushed or pulled?
Or told a rival story?

29. Good Friday

Does He ever wish He hadn't bothered? Are we really worthy of the sacrifice He made for us, allowing Himself to be humiliated and crucified, like a common criminal, so that we could make a fresh start with all our sins laid to rest?

What fresh start? We've just carried on the way we always did – squabbling and fighting, maiming and killing, lying and cheating, exploiting and abusing, indulging self while neglecting others, promoting unfairness and injustice …The list goes on.

If ***I*** had sacrificed myself I would expect a much better response than this. ***I*** would certainly wish I hadn't bothered!

But then, *I'm* not God!

30. A Mother's Pain

(This was written for a Good Friday service. The theme was "brokenness" and I was asked to write a poem from Mary's viewpoint as she stood looking at her son nailed to the cross)

How can it be? Reduced to this!
My son, my pride and joy
Betrayed, condemned, then crucified
My precious, darling boy

My son, so strong, so full of life
So gentle, kind and good
Destroyed, weak, helpless, left to die
Nailed to a cross of wood

His broken body scorned and mocked
What harm's He ever done?
What need was there to crush Him so?
My just and loving son

31. Easter Hope

A time for renewal, encouragement, joy
A time to reflect and take heart
A comforting time as we grow in our faith
- Perhaps time to make a fresh start

Our wrongs are forgiven. There's hope for us all
God loves us, whatever we do
Death isn't the end. We continue to live
God's with us our whole journey through

32. Easter Joy

An empty tomb, new life, new hope –
Rejoice with every breath
Our sins have been forgiven and
The Lord has conquered death

Today the world has been released
From fear of death's dark prison
For Jesus, who was crucified
Still lives – the Lord is risen!

So no more gloom, despair or doubt
Be filled with faith and joy
We have a living Saviour's love
Which *nothing* can destroy

33. Making Sense Of Easter

I must admit it troubles me
When thinking of this season
- If asked why it's important
Could I put in words the reason?

I know it in my heart and mind
But have I grasped it really?
How deeply do I understand?
Could I explain it clearly?

God came to earth in human form
- His name, of course, was Jesus -
To teach and guide and show the way
To challenge us. - And tease us?

Now human life was in a mess
Mistakes and crimes committed
So Jesus took these on Himself
That we might be acquitted

He gathered up and bore all sins
- A form of mediation -
To crucifixion on the cross
His death was our salvation

He died and, with Him, human wrongs
A fresh new start was waiting
Released from guilt, we're cleansed, reborn
That's why we're celebrating

And yet He wasn't really dead
He rose, to show He's living
- Death's not the end. We just move on
And God keeps on forgiving

34. Job Done
(*The Ascension*)

The Resurrection – what a thrill!
They'd seen Him crucified
They'd watched Him die. They'd placed Him
In a tomb. They'd mourned and cried

And then He rose! A miracle!
He wasn't dead at all!
They saw Him. He appeared to them
What rapture to recall!

And then He disappeared again
With promise to return
Though not in flesh. In spirit form
- He knew in time they'd learn

His job was done. He'd shown them
He was still alive, though "dead"
So home He went and left them
To consider what He'd said

35. Wind And Fire
(*Pentecost*)

In rush of wind and tongues of fire
The Holy Spirit came
Descending on those gathered there
In mighty gust and flame

No longer trapped in human form
Or tied to time or place
The Lord was once more with them
Though they couldn't see His face

His Spirit made them linguists all
Communicating well
With courage and conviction
And exciting news to tell

He lives within us, guiding us
He's in the air around
He's *everywhere*, each moment
Where we seek Him He'll be found

36. The Trinity

Father, Son and Holy Spirit
Three in one and one in three
Hard to grasp – yet not so really
Clues abound for all to see …

Woman – doctor, blogger, preacher
Little girl – niece, skater, friend
Different functions, all one person
This we surely comprehend

Man – proud parent, golfer, teacher
Boy – musician, gymnast, scout
Different functions, all one person
That's quite clear. We're in no doubt

Father, Son and Holy Spirit
Three in one and one in three
Different functions, all one Being
God – the Holy Trinity

37. Harvest Festival

Bountiful God, merciful Lord
Thank you for all that you give
Earth, seeds and harvests, sunshine and rain
Everything needed to live

Thank you for crops, plentiful, rich
Food in abundance each day
Clean wholesome water, wide-ranging goods
Thanks for this splendid display

38. Harvest Bounty

I celebrate harvest with gladness
The festival thrills me right through
That splendid arrangement of produce
The scents and the atmosphere too

I worship with hearty approval
And belt out the hymns till I'm hoarse
Oh yes, I rejoice in the harvest
- Though give little thought to its source

God's bounty is easy to come by
To me, here in Britain, at least
No shortage of food in *my* cupboards
Each day I face feast after feast

I know what I like, what I fancy
When thwarted I'm filled with disgust
- How *dare* they run out of my cookies?
What use is a shop I can't trust?

I hate to be hungry - well, peckish
And don't like to wait for my meal
Yet still I'll be fussy and choosy
No matter how empty I feel

You could say I'm just too complacent
To know what the festival means
Too lacking in true understanding
Too spoilt to be grateful for greens

Let's celebrate harvest with gladness
And give thanks for each food-packed store
But also find ways for God's bounty
To get to the starving and poor

39. A Harvest Thought

Let's pause a moment, just to think
To wonder and reflect
On all the pleasures life affords
The blessings we expect

The things we take for granted –
Things we want and things we need
- Food, clothing, shelter, comfort, warmth
Rain, sunshine, earth and seed

Imagine life without our treats
How empty it would be!
No chocolate, grapes, ice cream or cake
No soothing cup of tea

And all those sounds, smells, sights that thrill
- Birds singing, flowers, trees
Frosts, sunsets, rainbows, autumn hues –
God gave us *all* of these

So let's enjoy, with thankful hearts
The treasures that abound
And pray that soon we'll find a way
To *share* God's gifts around

40. A Harvest Prayer

We know of the hardship
The famine and drought
Poor harvests, starvation, despair
We're filled with compassion
And anger and rage
We know it's unjust and unfair

We know of the plenty
The wealth and the waste
The selfish indulgence and greed
We often feel guilty
For having so much
While others are dying in need

We know this imbalance
Is shameful and wrong
We know there's enough to go round
But knowing the problem
Achieves nothing good
If no sound solution is found

Please guide us – we're struggling
We really do care
But just can't see what can be done
To share out your bounty
Please help us to know
That war against want *can* be won

41. An Advent Prayer

Please help me keep things in perspective
As Christmas approaches once more
Reflecting on stable and manger
Remembering what it's all for
Please help me stay calm and unselfish
However much pressure there be
Above all, please help me remember
That Christmas is *not* about me

42. Waiting
(*Advent*)

Am I waiting for His coming?
Am I thinking of His birth?
Will I understand its meaning
For a deeply troubled earth?

Am I open to His message?
Will I take it to my heart?
Will I grow in loving kindness
Pray for peace and play my part?

Am I ready for His Coming?
Am I conscious of my need?
Will I feel His holy presence
In a world of sin and greed?

43. The Age-Old Story

That age-old Christmas story
We've heard it all before
The baby in the manger
- Can He tell us any more?

The shepherds and the angels
The wonder and the fear
The strange though joyful tidings
- Is there any more to hear?

The Wise Men on their journey
The star that led the way
The gifts and acts of homage
- Is there any more to say?

A baby born to save us
And teach us how to grow
To guide us by example
- Is there any more to know?

A man so full of goodness
Destroyed by human hand
God crucified, yet living
- Is there more to understand?

That age-old Christmas story
We've heard it all before
- But have we grasped its meaning?
Can it tell us something more?

44. Living Love

Can we really do it? Can we really make a difference if we take Love seriously? Are we even *capable* of taking Love seriously? Love requires us to be patient, respectful, tolerant, compassionate, considerate, unselfish, forgiving. Vengeance doesn't sit comfortably with Love. Neither does ruthlessness.

How often in our daily lives do we quibble over trivial matters? How often do we squabble, insist on having our say, refuse to back down because we know we're right? And how often does our behaviour cause bad feeling and unpleasantness?

We don't set out to upset anyone, as a general rule, or to provoke an argument, but we still manage to do it. For the most part, we are peaceful and well-meaning. We simply lack the grace and self-control to contain ourselves. We don't want to be misunderstood. We don't want to be pushed around. We don't want to take the blame for something that isn't our fault. There's usually a good reason - or excuse - for our insensitive behaviour towards others, but where are patience, respect, tolerance, compassion, consideration, selflessness and forgiveness in our need to have the last word and in our desire to get our own way?

Is it really any surprise that there is so much cruelty, inhumanity and unnecessary suffering in the world when peaceful, well-meaning people can't even live Love within their own families and communities?

Let's make a special effort from now on. Let's take Love seriously. Let's live Love and make a difference! We can do it - if we really want to.

45. The Christmas Message

Let's live the Christmas message
And let the whole world know
Let's make it real
And truly feel
The love we ought to show
Let's live the Christmas message
And rise above our woes
Be peaceful, kind
Of caring mind
Make friends instead of foes
Let's live the Christmas message
And put an end to strife
With love our guide
We'll turn the tide
And bring goodwill to life

46. God's Gift

God sent His Son, a gift of love
To show us how to live
- To treat with kindness all around
Be caring and forgive

God sent His Son to bring us peace
To help us understand
The need for calm and tolerance
Respect for every land

God sent His Son to spread goodwill
- Our hearts have room for all -
So let's give thanks and greet with joy
The baby in the stall

47. Getting It Right

Every Christmas I vow to get it right.

I will NOT get bogged down with practicalities and lose sight of its real meaning. I will NOT get fretful when things go wrong. I will NOT make Christmas all about me and how I feel and what I want.

I will make time during Advent to prepare properly, spiritually. I will soak up the thrill of the season and wake up on Christmas morning with a true sense of joy and wonder.

Yet every Christmas I get it wrong. I focus on the practicalities to the exclusion of anything spiritual. To my intense frustration and disappointment, I never seem to feel quite ready for the Carol Service, an important event in my anticipation of Christmas. I overreact to the slightest hiccup, declaring melodramatically that "Christmas is ruined". Even if I manage to keep a few days clear for calm reflection something will invariably crop up that demands my full attention or drains me emotionally. So still I fail to tune myself in properly to Christmas.

Life has taught me that if I don't feel "Christmassy" in the lead-up to Christmas I won't suddenly feel "Christmassy" when the day arrives either, and my longing to relax and enjoy the Twelve Days of Christmas will not be fulfilled.

It's easy to blame external forces and pressures for my difficulty in tuning into Christmas, but I know the problem is within me. I don't prepare properly and then I miss Christmas. I observe it, but I don't experience it, and then I feel empty and cheated.

I long so desperately to get it right and yet, year after year, I get it wrong.

Will I ever get it right?

48. No Room For Christmas

There's no room for Christmas
I can't fit it in
The season's so busy
My head's in a spin

With normal commitments
And presents to buy
Plus life's daily pressures
The time seems to fly

The cards still need writing
And posting – more cost
I've worked out my budget
But somewhere got lost

I'm late with the trimmings
The house looks quite bare
...A day or two more
And I think I'll be there

I've gifts to deliver
And people to see
A lunch with some friends
From eleven till three

There's no room for Christmas
No chance to reflect
I push it aside
Then miss out and object

It's not that my timetable's
Full, with no gaps
I'm just low in stamina
- Lazy, perhaps

A service of carols
Should focus my mind
- And surely it will
Once I've time to unwind

The big day approaches
I'm still in a flap
With Christmas Eve baking
And parcels to wrap

But when Christmas dawns
I'll be calmer, I know
The jobs will be done
And the pace will be slow

And, yes, so it is
I enjoy the whole day
- Church, presents and food -
In my own special way

I'll find room for Christmas
It's really begun
I'll soak up its message
Relax and have fun…

…From Boxing Day onwards
I feel strangely flat
For Christmas is over
The world tells me that

No long-lasting joy
Those twelve days are a con
The street's switched off Christmas
The atmosphere's gone

There's no point in hoping
That if I just wait
I'll find room for Christmas
- I've left it too late

It started so early
With carols and trees
And cards in November
- What meaning in these?

The first of December
Wherever you turn
It’s Christmas - no chance
To look forward and yearn

No Advent to build on
No tidings to hail
As Christmas draws closer
It’s all rather stale

And when it arrives
The excitement has passed
The first day of Christmas
For most, is the last

49. Boxing Day Chunter

"Did you have a nice Christmas?"

I've been asked that three times already and it's only Boxing Day. I keep wanting to reply, "I'm *having* a nice Christmas. It's *still* Christmas", but I don't want to sound snooty or weird, so I just smile weakly and say, "Yes, lovely, thank you".

By Boxing Day - or at least by 27th December - Christmas *is* pretty well over for most people. The decorations start coming down. By New Year the street will probably be almost bereft of decorations.

This part of Christmas, after Christmas Day, really gets me down. Other people have moved on. It's over for another year, yet I cling to it, trying to keep alive a feeling that isn't there any more.

Christmas has only just started and already people are switching it off. That long lead-up through December is *Advent.* By the time Christmas actually arrives people have had their fill of it. They've been doing Christmas for weeks and then Christmas Day just finishes it off - and what a relief that it's over.

Christmas *starts* with Christmas Day.

When things have calmed down, that's a perfect time to relax and enjoy Christmas, but for most of us the indulgences of Christmas Day are the big climax and then it's finished.

What's it all about anyway? Presents? Overspending? Overeating? Drunkenness?

Love? Peace? Goodwill to all?

Why does everything have to be *before* Christmas these days? We wouldn't spend weeks celebrating the imminent arrival of a new baby and then lose all interest in the child once it's actually here. Yet that's what we do with Christmas.

Advent is the time for preparation. Preparation for the festivities? Yes, of course. Even the average devout Christian would admit that most of his or her Christmas preparation is about cards, presents, food and logistics rather than about anything more spiritual.

But surely preparing ourselves for the gift of love, which is central to the Christmas festival, is worth a bit of our precious time too, even for people who are not Christian. Surely we can spend some time reflecting on the gift of God coming into the world in human form to show us how to live appropriately, with compassion and respect for everyone. If we just focus on the superficial trivialities of Christmas, what do we gain from it, apart from extra weight, a few more bits and pieces to find homes for and a lot of financial worry?

If people want to put their decorations up at the beginning of December that's fine by me. I enjoy looking at the decorations, even though I don't feel Christmassy myself at that stage. Carol Services at the beginning of December? No. That's far too early for me. Yet it strikes me that people are quite happy to proclaim that Jesus is born three weeks before the official day, but wouldn't dream or doing so three days after - when, to my mind, it's more relevant.

Of course, if people want to do Christmas that way it's their choice, but it's so hard to carry on with Christmas when all around you have switched it off. If you start late - the traditional way - you miss out on Christmas. Christmas has changed. Society has changed it.

People who start on Christmas early have up to a month to enjoy it. Those of us who begin later struggle to get two weeks. We lose the last part of Christmas because others have tired of it and moved on.

So what do I do? Just go with the flow? After all, isn't it better to fit in and feel at one with my surroundings than to be at odds with them? I'm always being told that change is the way forward, and there's something wrong with me if I don't embrace it unquestioningly. So do I just go with the flow?

Or do I stick to what I feel is right and try to ignore what's going on around me?

Why does it upset me so much? Why do I care?

Why don't we save a few exciting things for *after* Christmas Day? We cram everything into the lead-up to Christmas and Christmas Day itself, and then there's nothing for afterwards. Even carol singing doesn't seem to continue afterwards these days. I'm sure we used to still sing carols after Christmas Day when I was younger.

One thing I do know is *my* decorations will be staying up until twelfth night!

50. Love's Gifts

The gift of love, love's gift of peace
Received anew each year
That gift of peace, so longed for
Gets mislaid and yet it's *here*

Love's gift of hope, hope's gift of joy
Uplifting and profound
Excitement, cheerful greetings
Kindly gestures all around

Surprising then - these precious gifts
So dear on Christmas Day
Are played with for a while
Then disregarded, thrown away

The world is *starved* of love, hope, joy
And peace that's just and true
God's gift of Christmas, sent to all
Should last the whole year through

Other Titles By Helen M. Clarke

Noah Gets It Right
15 poems retelling Bible stories in a light-hearted, colloquial style.

Another Move, Another Church
A series of rhyming, rhythmic poems depicting a year in the life of a small English church, seen through the eyes of the minister's teenage daughter.

Life's Wonders And Riches
40 rhyming, rhythmic poems - a mixture of light-hearted and serious - celebrating and reflecting on life.

Mince Pies And Paper Chains
A collection of 22 rhyming poems, 12 short stories and 6 miscellaneous prose pieces, all on a Christmas theme.

"With Love And Best Wishes..."
An affectionate skit on the round-robin Christmas letter.

Christmas Uncancelled
A gentle Christmas story, suitable for children and adults.
Christmas is going to be awful. Lynette's parents have gone on holiday and left her with old-fashioned Auntie Dorothy and pesky little Johnny. To make matters worse, the neighbours are acting strangely and Lynette is sure they're up to no good. Lynette prepares herself for a miserable time. She has no intention of even trying to enjoy herself. But will she really be able to stay grumpy throughout Christmas?

Canine Confusions And Feline Frustrations
A cat and dog saga told through the animals' emails.
Rescue dog Scruff has just moved into a new home, where resident cat Cleopatra reigns supreme. To Scruff's surprise, Cleopatra doesn't seem particularly thrilled to have him around. As Scruff and Cleopatra try to come to terms with their new living arrangements, Scruff exchanges emails with worldly-wise Maxie, his friend from the Pound, while Cleopatra corresponds with her devoted sister Tallulah.

In Praise Of Amelia
A novel. Suzanne is a misfit and a failure, Amelia a successful career woman with devoted family and a wide circle of friends. The two were bitter rivals at school. Now in their thirties, with a reunion looming, will they be able to put the past behind them? Or will old grievances and festering wounds be inflamed?

Verses For Greeting Cards
100 rhyming poems, with no copyright restrictions, for use in card making.

More Verses For Greeting Cards
A second collection of rhyming poems, with no copyright restrictions, for use in card making. A companion to the first collection.

Verses For Birthday And Christmas Cards
65 rhyming poems, with no copyright restrictions, for use in card making. There are 35 birthday verses (12 of which are for children) and 30 Christmas verses (6 for children).

Expert Menace
Satirical fiction in which experts who are a menace and people who are simply expert at *being* a menace feature strongly.

Delphinia's Magic
A spoof celebrity memoir.

Prowlers In the Moonlight
A children's mystery story. There are strange goings-on in a quiet little village. Kelly, Michael and Kathryn decide to investigate.

One More Story...And Another...And Another
Stories and poems for young children.

24474945R00033

Printed in Great Britain
by Amazon